The 8th Wave

James Ernest

Published by Playdead Press 2013

© James Ernest

James Ernest has asserted his rights under the Copyright, Design and Patents Act, 1988, to be identified as the author of this work.

A CIP catalogue record for this book is available from the British Library.

ISBN 978-0-9576077-2-9

Caution
All rights whatsoever in this play are strictly reserved and application for performance should be sought through the author before rehearsals begin. No performance may be given unless a license has been obtained.

This book is sold subject to the condition that it shall not by way of trade or otherwise, be lent, resold, hired out, or otherwise circulated without the publisher's prior consent in any form of binding or cover other than that in which it is published and without a similar condition including this condition being imposed on the subsequent purchaser.

Playdead Press
www.playdeadpress.com

For my Grandma and Grandad

The 8th Wave was written by James Ernest in Spring and Summer 2012 and was runner-up in Soho Theatre's Soho Young Writers' Award the same year.

It was previewed at Dyspla Festival at the Tristan Bates Theatre, London, 7th-10th November 2012.

Mathew	Alex Payne
Brian	Francis Adams
Director	Don Mc Camphill
Designer	Konrad Haller
Set assistant	Dominik Gieryn
Video artist	Caroline Chang

The play was subsequently optioned by Disturbance production company.

It opened for its first run at The Space, London, on 2nd April 2013.

Mathew	Alex Payne
Brian	Francis Adams
Directors	Don Mc Camphill, Luke Lutterer
Producer	Nick Rushton
Designer	Konrad Haller
Education associate	Jackie Kearns
Graphic designer	Chris Lovell

Foreword

At Soho Theatre, when I ran the Young Writers' Programmes there, we had regular rehearsed reading slots, and many good writers had their debuts there: Inua Ellams, Rachel Briscoe, Maeve Mc Keown, Natalie Mitchell, Peter Cant. Not all of them went on to become professional writers, but many did, and all have made important contributions to contemporary British Theatre.

James Ernest joined the Young Writers' Programme in early 2012 where he wrote *The 8th Wave*, his first full length play. At the next rehearsed reading in Soho Theatre Upstairs, *The 8th Wave* was on the bill. James subsequently developed the play, with support and feedback from the team, and submitted it for the inaugural Soho Young Writers' Award, where it was a runner up and received a Special Commendation.

When I left Soho Theatre to set up Disturbance, James' play was one of two I optioned with a view to producing. It exactly fitted the new company's brand: it was original, socially engaged, theatrical. It challenged received wisdoms, it dealt with intriguing characters in thorny situations, and it had something interesting to say. It was in its way unsettling for the reader, and would be stimulating for an audience.

Beyond that, we had a very clear view of where we wanted to position ourselves as a company. With the economic collapse, some bigger theatres were playing safer with programming, or not risking new work. New writing theatres were looking for tried and tested pieces that had already built an audience or new work that had co-production possibilities. We felt sure that good writers would be overlooked, and we wanted to be there to pick them up. Again James fitted the bill. He is just the sort of writer we were interested in developing, with just the sort of play we wanted to produce: a play that challenged audiences, but also rewards them.

We hope you find the play as rewarding to read as it has been for us to produce.

Don Mc Camphill - March 2013

Characters

Mathew – a white, British male in his early twenties.

Brian – a white, British male in his mid/late fifties.

Notes

/
An interruption.

…
Lost in thought or a loss of words.

Setting

An independent business in a ruinous seaside town.
It is two o'clock in the morning.

Mathew is strapped tightly to a wooden chair with rope.
We can barely see him, because of the darkness.

Within the darkness we see a small wooden table and an old wooden chair.
On the table there is a daily newspaper.

The Third Wave

Brian enters.
He is wearing a pair of old underwear, a white vest top and his dressing gown.
We hear the sound of his slippers, dragging along against the ground as he walks.
He is holding a bowl of beans in one hand and a spoon in the other.
He places them onto the table and then, he leaves.

After sometime, Brian enters with a glass jug full of water in one hand and an empty glass in the other.
He walks to the table.
He fills the empty glass with water.
He exits with the jug of water.

Pause.

Brian enters again.
He has a side plate in his hand, on it, two slices of bread, buttered.
He walks to the table and he places the plate down onto it.
He takes his slippers off and places them in their usual spot.
He sits on the wooden chair.
He takes a drink of his water and places the glass back onto the table, in its usual spot.
He picks up a slice of bread.

We instantly hear a small buzzing noise.
Brian freezes.
We see a small fly cross the stage.
Brian follows the fly closely with his eyes.
The fly exits.
The sound fades.

Short pause.

Brian dips the bread into the beans.
We hear the same buzzing noise.
Brian freezes.
We see the same fly cross the stage.
Brian follows the fly closely with his eyes.
The fly exits.
The sound fades.

Pause.

He begins to eat.

BRIAN: Each morning, they wake me up with their inconsiderate buzzing, wanting, waiting for me to open the window so that they can escape.
I never open the window.
Instead I make myself a cup of tea, no milk, no sugar.
I read the daily newspaper.
The mirror, the sun, they are all the same.
Same sort of stories with similar endings.
And when I'm done I roll it up and I swat the little fuckers.
I don't know how they manage to get in, I don't think they know.
They don't think I see them, shitting on everything they touch, I see them, I observe them, and then I make sure.
I make sure they don't have the chance to do it again.
The next morning, the same, always the same, they never learn.
Instead they shit.
They shit on everything they can.

Short pause.

BRIAN: This is nice.
A nice treat.
Are you hungry?

Mathew is silent.

BRIAN: If you're hungry, all you have to do is say.

Brian takes another bite.

BRIAN: Oh this is nice.
Always enjoyed beans with bread me, ever since I was a kidder.
My favorite meal actually.
If I were particularly good, I would be given a bowl of beans and 2 slices of bread for breakfast, lunch and dinner.
I never really enjoyed toast.
Too rough for my liking.

Mathew is silent.

BRIAN: When was the last time you ate?

Mathew is silent.

BRIAN: You look hungry.

Mathew is still silent.

BRIAN: Are you?

Silent.

BRIAN: Oh, the silent treatment.
I remember this game very well.

Silent.

BRIAN: Moping are we?
Sulking are we?
In a huff are we?
Moody are we?
Down in the...

MATHEW: I'm not hungry.

BRIAN: Suit yourself.

Pause.

BRIAN: Do you smoke?

MATHEW: These days, everybody smokes.

Brian takes out a packet of cigarettes from his dressing gown pocket.
He walks towards Mathew.
He places one cigarette into the mouth of Mathew.

BRIAN: There we are.

Brian places the cigarettes back into his pocket.
He takes a box of matches from his pocket, he strikes one and he lights the cigarette for Mathew.

BRIAN: And. Off. We. Go.
Better?

He places the matches back into his pocket.
Brian begins to stroke Mathew's hair.
He is gentle.

He almost immediately stops.

Brian takes the cigarette out of the Mathew's mouth and looks at it.

BRIAN: I enjoy a good cigarette after I've eaten.

Brian smokes.
He feels the smoke deep inside him.
He blows the smoke in the air.
The smoke fills the stage.
He observes it.

BRIAN: It's suffocating isn't it?
I can feel it, here, clinging to me like a lost child.
Lots of small hopeless children.
I can feel it, pulling me.
It wants me to help it, to keep it, to need it.
It is addictive.

He takes another drag.
He blows the smoke into the air again.
He observes it.

BRIAN: Did you know, smoking a single cigarette reduces your life expectancy by eleven minutes?

He looks at the cigarette and then he places it onto the side plate.

BRIAN: It amuses me.

MATHEW: What?

BRIAN: Don't you find it funny?

MATHEW: No, I don't.

BRIAN: We are choosing to smoke aren't we?
It is a decision made by ourselves, we are making a choice.
We choose to suffocate ourselves.
We are choosing pain and disease.
We are embracing illness with open arms and we are choosing death over life.
Isn't that fascinating?

Short pause.

BRIAN: How much?

MATHEW: What?

BRIAN: How much do you smoke?

MATHEW: It depends.

BRIAN: On what?

MATHEW: I don't know.

BRIAN: The day?
The mood?
The weather?

MATHEW: The mood.

BRIAN: Your mood or the mood of others?

MATHEW: Mine.

BRIAN: And do you feel the rush?

MATHEW: The what?

BRIAN: Do you smoke to feel something?

MATHEW: Sometimes.

BRIAN: So, do you feel the rush?

MATHEW: Now and then, yes.

BRIAN: Sometimes he smokes to…
When did you start smoking?

MATHEW: I was fifteen.

BRIAN: And now you're twenty?

MATHEW: I'm twenty-two.

BRIAN: Right.
You're twenty-two, yes.
Right.
You look younger.

Short pause.

BRIAN: So, let's say you smoke, on average, five cigarettes a day.
Now I know it is probably more, it is isn't it?
But, let's just say for the purpose of this conversation that you smoked 5 cigarettes a day for seven years.
Now that is five, eleven, three six five.
Including the leap year.
One point eight two five.
Twelve point seven seven five.

Eight point three four two.
Ninety-seven.
Ninety-eight.
You have lost ninety-eight days already.
Approximately, in 7 years.
It is probably more.
Most defiantly, depending whether or not five is the correct figure.

Short pause.

BRIAN: And is that why you smoke?

Mathew is silent.

BRIAN: Well, you smoke for the rush, and sometimes you get it and sometimes you don't.
So, you smoke, and you wait.
You light up a cigarette and you wait for the rush, and when it doesn't give you what you want, you are left disappointed.
Wanting, right?

MATHEW: No.
I don't *just* smoke for the rush.

BRIAN: Why then?
The burn?

MATHEW: Boredom.
It entertains me.

BRIAN: Ah!
It entertains your fingers.

MATHEW: You could say that, yes.

BRIAN: So, you could say that it amuses you also?

Pause.

Brian stares at Mathew.
He stands.
Brian takes his old wooden chair and places near Mathew.
He sits and continues to stare.

BRIAN: Are you ill?
You are ill.
You look ill.

MATHEW: I am.

BRIAN: You are?

MATHEW: Yes.
Yes, I am.

BRIAN: You look ill.
Medically?

MATHEW: I suppose.

BRIAN: What do the doctors say?

MATHEW: I don't talk doctors.

BRIAN: Why?

Short pause.

MATHEW: When I was younger / I was…

BRIAN: / You were ill?

MATHEW: Yes.

BRIAN: Very ill?
Or did you have a cold?

MATHEW: Very.
I shit the bed.

BRIAN: Where were you?

MATHEW: I was in my bed.

BRIAN: That makes sense.
Did you call the doctors?

MATHEW: I was too ill to move
My mother called them.

BRIAN: Did she?
She called the doctors for you did she?

MATHEW: Yes.
She had to.

BRIAN: And what did they do?
Did they help?

MATHEW: They gave me meds.
Came to my house and said I had to take them.
They said if I did, they would make me better.

BRIAN: And did they work?
The meds?

MATHEW: I hate tablets so I never took them.
My step dad tried to make me.

BRIAN: Did he?

MATHEW: Yes, he would try to force me.
When he left my room I pushed my fingers to the back of my throat.
And he never knew.

They come back, the doctors, and they look at me.
"You're better now."
Yes, I was better, but I never took them.
What was that all about then, the meds?

And that's why I don't talk to doctors anymore.
I don't / trust them.

BRIAN: / You don't trust them.

Brian places his chair next to Mathew.

Short pause.

BRIAN: Then how do you know?

MATHEW: I'm sick.
I smoke and I am sick.
I'm sick and then I smoke.
And then / I'm sick.

BRIAN: / You're sick.

Short pause.

BRIAN: Do you enjoy the smoke?
Suffocating?
Do you enjoy that?

MATHEW: It sort of sooths me.
I feel it circulating.
The smoke calms me.

BRIAN: What about the smell?

MATHEW: On the fingers?

BRIAN: And on your clothes.

MATHEW: I hate the smell.

BRIAN: The scent of rot.

MATHEW: I hate it.

BRIAN: When the smoke has gone, but the smell remains, what do you do?

MATHEW: I feel numb.

BRIAN: Yes, but what do you do?

MATHEW: Sometimes I struggle.

BRIAN: You struggle?

MATHEW: Sometimes I struggle to breathe.

BRIAN: And that is when you fight?

MATHEW: I, yes.

BRIAN: To stay?

MATHEW: Yes.

BRIAN: Here?

Mathew *is silent.*

BRIAN: I think I understand.

Silence.

MATHEW: What time is it?

BRIAN: Half past two.

MATHEW: I need to piss.

BRIAN: You need to…
Right, he needs to…
Right.
Ok.

Brian picks up the glass of water and he drinks the remainder of the water.
He rushes over to Mathew.
He crouches in front of him with the empty glass.
He unbuttons Mathew's trousers.

MATHEW: What, what the fuck are / you doing?

BRIAN: / Just stay calm.

He puts his hand into Mathew's trousers.

MATHEW: Get your fucking hand out of my…
Oh god.

Brian takes out Mathew's penis and places it into the glass.

MATHEW: Get the fuck / off!

BRIAN: / Piss.

MATHEW: Stop it.

BRIAN: You need a piss don't you?
/ Piss.

MATHEW: / Stop it.
Leave it alone.

BRIAN: I have things to do.
I have to pack.
I'm not looking.

MATHEW: Get your hand off my / dick.

BRIAN: / You said you need to piss?

MATHEW: I DO!

BRIAN: THERE'S NO NEED TO RAISE YOUR VOICE!

MATHEW: Take my cock out of the glass, untie me and let me use the bog.

BRIAN: Right then.

He throws the glass on the floor.
It smashes.

BRIAN: Right, fine.
Yes.

Brian places Mathew's penis back into his trousers.

BRIAN: Try not to piss on my floor

He walks over to the wooden table.
He puts on his slippers.
He picks up the newspaper.
Brian looks at Mathew.

BRIAN: Won't you scream?

MATHEW: No.
It wouldn't help the situation.

BRIAN: What situation?

MATHEW: This situation.

BRIAN: Oh, this situation.
You would be heard.
Someone would be bound to hear.

MATHEW: No, nobody would.

BRIAN: Someone would.

MATHEW: You would gag me.

BRIAN: After a while.
I thought you were rebellious.
If you want to be saved, shout!
If you want help / then scream.

MATHEW: / I don't want help.
I never said I wanted help.

BRIAN: Cry for somebody to rescue you.
If you are scared, yelp!

MATHEW: I'm not scared.

BRIAN: Go on!
Cry for the police to rescue / you.

MATHEW: / No!

BRIAN: You're not going to try?

Mathew is silent.

BRIAN: He is not going to / try.

MATHEW: / Your neighbors would wake up.
They would put in their earphones, roll over and then fall back to sleep.
They wouldn't get involved.

In the morning, your neighbor's wouldn't remember the shouting.
Why should they?
People have arguments all the time these days.
People scream at the top of their voices.
People throw things.

They explode.

Your neighbors will ignore.
They would forget.
Pay no attention / to...

BRIAN: / You're silenced.
You want to scream, but you will not admit it.
You won't scream because you want to breath.
You want somebody to listen but you believe they won't listen.
You surprise me.
I thought I knew you.
I would like to know you.
A little bit of you.
At least for a little while.

Pause.

BRIAN: I was bound to a chair once.
I can't remember my age exactly, maybe I was five?
Let's say I was five.

Mathew is silent.

BRIAN: I was at the dentist you see, having a tooth removed.
I lay on their bed.
My Mam was there holding my hand.
And there was a lady.
And I remember her smile, she had such a nice smile.
She asked me if I was ok.
I told her I was scared, because I was, I was terrified.
She said I was going to be fine.
She said everything was going to be ok.

Of course she did.
She put a mask on my face, the nurse.
I remember there being a tube connecting the mask to a machine.
The lady said I had to take deep breaths in.
So I did.
Mam was encouraging me.
She was squeezing my hand.
The air tasted of mint, the air coming from the mask.
And then I became dizzy, and I started to panic.
The more I took a breath in and then out, the dizzier I became and the more I panicked.
I was kicking, I tried to get up.
I tried to take the mask off but the lady forced me down, I couldn't move.
I tried to get up.
I did.
And then I remember looking at my Mam and she was helping, she was holding me down too.
I was screaming her name.
I was screaming Mum.
And that's all I can remember.
I must have fallen asleep.
I woke up and I didn't know where I was.
I tried to hate her for weeks afterwards.
But I couldn't.
It wasn't until a couple of years after that, I realized, it was for my own good.
She held me down because she was helping.

Short pause.

BRIAN: And now you're here, sat there.
This is for your own good.

Silence.

We hear a buzzing noise.
Brian freezes.
He turns.
The buzzing gets louder.
Irritating.
The fly enters the stage.
Brian follows the fly carefully with his eyes.
The fly lands on the table.
Brian swats the fly with the paper.

The Forth Wave.

Brian is sat at the wooden table.
The newspaper is open and he is playing Sudoku.
He has a pen in his hand.
The bowl of beans and the spoon has been removed.
The side plate still remains.

BRIAN: 8.

He thinks.

BRIAN: Forty-two.
Seven.

Short pause.

BRIAN: I always enjoyed maths.
Not many people did, but I loved it, sums, subtractions, and stuff like that.
Did you enjoy math's much?
My teacher always said I had a natural talent for multiplication.
I found it fun, numbers.
It was like learning another language.
I wasn't very good at French or German so I guess numbers were my specialty.
Communicating with numbers, moving them around, looking at equations in different ways in order to find the correct answer.
And that was the fun bit, finding the answer.
Yes it would frustrate me sometimes when I couldn't find...
And the...

But I would feel challenged, mentally exhausted sometimes, but when I found the answer…
All the other kids would laugh at me for putting my hand up, for giving the right answer.
They would call me names.
But I didn't care because I felt like a wizard.
She would call me that sometimes, my teacher, a mathematical wizard.

He folds the newspaper and places it in front of him on the table.
The pen goes on top.

BRIAN: Did you enjoy Math's?

MATHEW: Math?
No.

BRIAN: What about English?

MATHEW: Bits of it.

BRIAN: What bits?

MATHEW: Poetry.

BRIAN: I don't like poetry.
I never really understood it.
They make it far too complicated you know.
I mean why don't people just say what they want to say?
Rather than trying to make it sound pretty.
That's all they do you know, they decorate the basic message.
They pollute it.
Poetry.

You can't do much with poetry.
It's useless.

Short pause.

BRIAN: Wait here.

MATHEW: Where are you going?

BRIAN: Just stay here.

Brian leaves the room.

Mathew makes a decision.
Mathew begins to struggle.
He tries to twist his hands through the rope.
He ignores the pain.
He battles.
He is desperate.
He keeps his eyes on the door at all times.
Brian returns.
He is excited.
Mathew suddenly becomes still.
In one hand Brian has a small wooden boat.
In the other, he has a small pot of white paint and a paintbrush.

BRIAN: Look!

Brian holds the boat up high.

BRIAN: Here we are.
This.
I made this.
Now that was a great lesson.

MATHEW: It's good.

BRIAN: I know.
Did you enjoy it?

MATHEW: D and T?

BRIAN: No, woodwork?

MATHEW: I wasn't very good.

BRIAN: That's a shame isn't it?
You could have made something like this.
I remember the day I finished making it actually.
I was twelve.
It was Friday.
But this day I knew I had to finish it.
I knew I had to finish it, because it was Dad's birthday, so it had to be done that day.
I still had a lot of work to do, the final details.
I had to sand it, and paint it, then varnish the thing.
I only had time to sand the boat.
You know, I made it look presentable, so I could give it to my Dad for his present.
And then I thought, maybe, we could paint it together, at home.
And varnish it, of Corse.
The bell rang at school and I rushed home to show my Dad.
When I got there, Mam was in the kitchen.
I ran up to her and I held it up, like this.
She looked at the boat and then back at me and she could see how happy I was.
She smiled and she gave me the biggest hug.
She was so proud of me, you could tell, her face was so…

I asked her where Dad was, she said he was still at work, so I waited in the living room all night until he arrived home.
It got to 8pm and he still wasn't home.
This was way past my bedtime, but Mam could see how much it meant to me so she let me stay up late.

Short pause.

BRIAN: At nine, I heard the door open.
I ran to the door with the boat in my hand and he was stood there, with a smile on his face and his arms wide open for me.
We played with the boat until eleven that night, all of us, me, my Mam and my Dad.

Brian smiles.
He takes the newspaper from the wooden table and places it onto the floor.
He places the boat onto it.

BRIAN: I loved my Mam very much.

MATHEW: And your Father?

BRIAN: Everybody loves their Father.

MATHEW: Do they?

Brian sits down on the floor, beside the boat.

BRIAN: Oh yes, it's obligatory.
You have to....
You never stop loving your Father.
I could never stop.

There is a sound of a gastropod shell being blown from the outside.

Short pause.

Brian starts to paint the wooden boat.

MATHEW: You said you needed to pack.

Brian is painting his boat.

MATHEW: Earlier, you said you needed to pack.
You said you needed to pack your suitcase?

BRIAN: Yes, I do.
I do need to, yes.

Brian continues to paint.

MATHEW: So, you are going on holiday?

Brian continues.

MATHEW: Are you going / on holiday?

BRIAN: Yes.
Yes, a holiday.

MATHEW: That sounds nice.

BRIAN: It is.

MATHEW: Is it?

BRIAN: Yes.
Very nice.

Brian continues to paint.

MATHEW: The morning fog is close.
We don't get much sun at all, do we?
Always seems to be grey.
But when we do get sun, I love it.
I go down to the beach.
Do you?

BRIAN: Not anymore.

MATHEW: Not even when it's sunny?

BRIAN: I never really enjoyed the sun that much.

The gastropod shell sounds again.

Short pause.

Brian continues to paint the boat.

MATHEW: Where you are going?
Will you leaving the shop behind?

Brian paints.

MATHEW: How long are you going / away for?

BRIAN: / If you looked at the notice on the front door before you rudely broke in, you would have known that I'm going away for some time.

Short pause.

BRIAN: What do you want?
Why are you asking so many questions?

MATHEW: They are friendly / questions.

BRIAN: / Yes, but why?
Why are you asking so many questions?
I am trying to concentrate.
Right now, all I want to do is paint my boat.

Short pause.

MATHEW: I'm sorry.

Brian continues to paint his boat.

MATHEW: I'm sorry I interrupted you and your boat painting.

Short pause.

MATHEW: I just need to / know something.

BRIAN: / You do not *need* to know anything.
You are asking because you would *like* to know something?
Correct?

Brian stares at Mathew.

BRIAN: And what would you like to know exactly?
What would you like to know?

Short pause.

MATHEW: You won't be opening the shop today, will you?

BRIAN: No.
I won't be opening today.
Or tomorrow.

Brian stands.

BRIAN: I need to finish packing.

Brian begins to walk away.

MATHEW: Aren't you worried it will happen again?
When you're away, somebody may see that sign.
You won't be home and it could happen again.

BRIAN: It won't happen again.

MATHEW: How do you know it won't?
Aren't you worried?

BRIAN: It won't happen again.

MATHEW: You don't know that.
You don't.
You could hire somebody to run it for you?

BRIAN: What?

MATHEW: Somebody to take care of this / place for you.

BRIAN: / What are you trying?

MATHEW: There are lots of people out there looking for a job.

BRIAN: Lots of people?
Looking?
Like you?

MATHEW: I could do it.

The gastropod shell sounds again.

BRIAN: I knew it was just a matter of time.
I knew you / would try something.

MATHEW: / I'd work hard.
I could run the shop, for you, until you get back?
I'm a fast learner.
I could look after your customers.
I could clean the place for you too.
I would do it for you.
Help you.

BRIAN: You want to run it for me?
You want to be in charge?

MATHEW: Yes, I could / do it.

BRIAN: / Have you had any experience?

MATHEW: Working in a shop?

BRIAN: Yes.
Have you had any managerial experience?

MATHEW: No, I don't.

BRIAN: But you have worked in a shop?

MATHEW: No, I haven't.
But like I said, I am a quick learner.
I learn things, fast.
Pick up things really / easily.

BRIAN: / When I was younger I remember my Father had an old conch shell, it was his childhood item.

MATHEW: What?

BRIAN: You know these days people keep an item don't they, to remind them, so that they can cling on.
And he kept this item inside of his room,
I was never allowed to play on it.
He cherished it.
It was too precious to him I guess.
He played it.
It made the most beautiful sound.
I think it was his Father's.
It must have been.
I was allowed to stroke it, and listen to it, but I was never allowed to play it.
I always wanted to, it was very tempting.
You always want to do what you cannot.
He took good care of that too, polished it, cleaned it, treat it nicely.
I always wished that he would give me it one day, when he was too old and he couldn't take care of it.

The day he died I remember going into his room, I walked up to it, and I placed my lips closely to its...
But I couldn't do it, it didn't seem right.
It felt wrong.

My Mother died shortly afterwards, and she left me the house and everything in it.
A few years later, I sold the house and I the conch shell and I bought this shop.
A shop on the sea front.
This is what I treasure, something I can take care of.
Something I can look after and love.

Brian takes a cigarette from his pocket and observes it.

BRIAN: Nineteen years it's taken me, to get this place into shape.
Built it up.
When I got it, it was empty.
Just four walls, and it has taken me this long.
It's my home now.
And when you broke your way in, I was shocked.
I was angry.
I didn't think that day would come.
I didn't think that day would come but I was prepared.
I have read about these things in the paper.
But I just don't get it.
People don't just come in here to shop you know.
They come in to see me, to say hello, to converse.
I'm nice, people come and say hello and talk to me because I'm nice.
I make them a cup of tea and they talk to me because I'm pleasant.
But when you broke in, it upset me, I got angry and I am not an angry person.
It's a good job I was awake.
You didn't see the light?
Didn't you know I was awake?
I heard you, smashing things.
Did you or did you not see the sign?

Or were you too busy with the brick in your hand?

Brian takes a match and lights the cigarette.
He smokes.

BRIAN: It's taken me nineteen years to get to where I am now and I couldn't let you get away.
I have worked too hard, and you think you can come in here and take anything you want?
This feels normal to you doesn't it?
It's just another day to you isn't it?
And that's why you're here.
I have to make sure you won't do it again.

MATHEW: Untie me.

BRIAN: *You* act as if these streets are your own and nobody else's.
You piss on the street corners.
You take and you abuse and you think there are no consequences?
I see little twats like you every day.
Fighting each other, killing each other and for what?
Just so you can take another step?
So you can smile?
You take great pleasure from this.

In yesterday's paper there was a picture of a boy who was beat down, he was bleeding from the nose.
And there was a picture in the paper of a man, I thought at first he was helping the boy up from the ground.
I read the article.
He wasn't helping him, he was mugging him.
He was taking from the bag, the boy didn't know, he was in shock the poor lad.

The man was taking things out of the bag and he was smiling.
It makes me feel sick.
And nobody was there to stop him, the twat, there was nobody there to say no.

Brian puts the cigarette out.

BRIAN: When you're younger you get a slap on the hand don't you?
Then you instantly know the thing you did was wrong.
When you grow up you forget that.
You forget about the slap.
Or maybe you don't?
Maybe you know the thing you're doing *is* wrong, but there is nobody there to slap.
Maybe that's it?
We all need somebody there to say no.
To slap.
And that's why I'm doing this, I'm slapping, I'm saying / no!

MATHEW: / I said un-fucking-tie me!
I want to go now.

BRIAN: I'm teaching you / a lesson.

MATHEW: / I want to go.

BRIAN: I'm going to help you.

MATHEW: I don't want help.

BRIAN: Don't you see?
You have a choice.

I'm teaching you.
I'm trying to help you / to understand.

MATHEW: / No you're not!
You can't teach me anything.

BRIAN: Why do you have to be so ignorant?
I am a nice guy.
I am /nice.

MATHEW: / Nice?

BRIAN: Yes.

MATHEW: Generous?

BRIAN: Some would say I am / generous.

MATHEW: / Lovely?

BRIAN: People in the past have described me as / lovely.

MATHEW: / Who?

BRIAN: What?

MATHEW: Who has ever called you lovely?

BRIAN: What?

MATHEW: Come on.
Who?

BRIAN: Look, the point I am trying to make / is that...

MATHEW: / I want to know.

BRIAN: The point is / that...

MATHEW: / I want some names.

BRIAN: There are lots of freaks out there.
I should know, I read about them.
Imagine if one of *them* caught you eh?
You'd be in a hell of a lot of trouble then.
You would be in a blender or something.

MATHEW: A blender?
You're not serious.
Pick up the phone and call the police.

BRIAN: The police?

MATHEW: Yes.

BRIAN: I could give up.
I could pick up the phone and call them.
And you would walk away and forget about the slap.

MATHEW: Pick up the phone and call the / police.

BRIAN: / But, I'm helping you.
The police won't / help you.

MATHEW: / Listen to me.

BRIAN: NO!
YOU HAVE A PROBLEM, IT IS YOU THAT NEEDS HELP.
You did what you did because it was a cry for help.

You were yelling for somebody to help.
I'm not going to give up on / you!

MATHEW: / FLIES SUCK.
They absorb, they suck and they feed.
They slurp their meals through their tongues.
A fly doesn't shit, it vomits.
It vomits enzymes and it vomits saliva.
You were wrong.
You can't teach me anything.
You are living a life that is repetitive and dull.
You talk *at* people to try and make *your* day worthwhile.
You belt the same tune over and over, just hoping that one-day they will believe what you tell them.

BRIAN: Don't you talk to me like that.

MATHEW: People don't come in here to see *you*, why would they?
They come in here because they know they'll get a free cupper.

BRIAN: You're not in the position to talk to me like that.

MATHEW: Your customers' smile at your stories, they nod in agreement at your judgments, they grit their teeth at your comments and then, when they have finished their drink, they leave.
To them you are a free hot beverage dispenser.
All I see is a sad, lonely old man, praying.
You're on your knees waiting for somebody to call you their / friend.

BRIAN: / Stop it!
You don't know me.

People know me.
My friends know me.
You little shit.
I do not talk *at* them.
I talk to them about things, important things.

MATHEW: That you read out of the paper?

BRIAN: STOP IT.
You little shit.
My friends know that I am interesting.
They know me, you don't.
People always smile and wave when they walk by.
People come in here not *just* to buy groceries, they come in to talk to me.
My friends come in here and they talk to me.
And they tell *me* things also, we converse.
We have very important conversations!
I am not a free beverage dispenser.
And I am not a machine!
I am not alone.
I am a person…
How dare you!
I'm not alone!
I'm not!
I AM NOT ALONE!

Complete silence.

BRIAN: You know what I should do?
I should punch you.
Kick you.
Slap you.
You know, that kind of thing.

MATHEW: You shouldn't do that.

BRIAN: Why shouldn't I?
There has to be a consequence.
Maybe I should stab you a little?
Maybe I should stab you a little in the arm, or the leg?

MATHEW: You don't want to do that.

BRIAN: No, I don't, but I think I should.

Brian picks up the largest shard of glass from the floor.

MATHEW: Don't do that.

BRIAN: Pain does that, doesn't it?
It tells you something.
It communicates.

Brian walks closer to Mathew.

BRIAN: It warns you, doesn't it?

MATHEW: Please.

Brian walks closer.

BRIAN: Just a little cut.
Just a little bit.
It wouldn't kill you.
I need to know that you care.
I need to know that you / understand.

MATHEW: / I care!
I do.

BRIAN: Is that what you are afraid of?
The pain.

MATHEW: Please, think about it.
Think about / what you are…

BRIAN: / If you're not afraid, then why are you squirming?
Your muscles are tense.
You are still.
Too still.
And your heart is throbbing, faster than before.

Brian moves closer.

MATHEW: I fucking care!
I do!

Brian circles Mathew.

BRIAN: Your foot maybe?
Would you mind if I stabbed your / foot?

MATHEW: / YES!

BRIAN: Keep the noise down.

Brian places the sharp glass onto Mathew's crotch.

BRIAN: How about / your cock?

MATHEW: / Yes.

Brian runs the piece of glass up to Mathew's neck.

MATHEW: Yes!
I would mind.

BRIAN: How will you learn?

MATHEW: I have learnt.

BRIAN: Your lesson?

MATHEW: A lesson, yes.

BRIAN: What have you learnt?

MATHEW: I've learnt / that...

Brian runs the glass over Mathew's shoulders and onto his back.
He presses down.

BRIAN: / In great detail.

MATHEW: Yes, ok, I have learnt / that...

BRIAN: / Maybe just a finger.

MATHEW: NO!
I have learnt that, that...
/ That...

BRIAN: / Just the little finger?

MATHEW: NO!
Please!
No.

BRIAN: You must hate yourself.

Brian removes the shard of glass from Mathew's back.

BRIAN: A little part of you.
You must want to cut yourself sometimes.
There must be a place inside you, a little place inside of yourself.
A little place that you yearn to tear out.
A little place…

Short pause.
Brian drops the piece of glass onto the floor.

BRIAN: I know I do.

Stillness.

The Fifth Wave.

Brian is packing his suitcase.
Beside him is a collection of items.
The collection includes a dark green diary, two shirts, one grey and one white, one pair of black trousers, a pair of pajamas, his favorite.
One pair of cream shorts, one pair of brown sandals, a pair of socks and an old brown hat.
Mathew is still sat in the chair, tied.

MATHEW: I've been in here before.
With my little brother.

BRIAN: I haven't seen you in here before.

MATHEW: We were very young then.
My mother left me fifty pence on the windowsill for some sweets.
And when I came in, I saw you there, behind the counter, and I gave you the money.

BRIAN: How old were you?

MATHEW: Young.
I gave you the money first.
Because that's what I thought you did, give the money first.

BRIAN: That's silly.

MATHEW: I was young, that's what I thought you did.
I went to the sweets and I picked my favorite, the sour ones.
The orange sours.
And then, I started to walk out.

BRIAN: I can't remember.

MATHEW: You came over and took the sweets out of my hands.
You threatened to call the police.

BRIAN: I did not.

MATHEW: You said, "They'll be after you".
You were angry.

BRIAN: I wouldn't say that.

MATHEW: You did.
I hadn't stolen.
I'd given you the money.

BRIAN: Why didn't you explain?

MATHEW: I didn't say anything because I was so scared.

BRIAN: You should have said.
You should have / explained.

MATHEW: / Do you remember?
I was only / young.

BRIAN: / How young?

MATHEW: I must have been eight.
You took me by the wrist and pulled me outside and told me never to come back. My brother was a mess.

BRIAN: Your little brother?

MATHEW: He didn't understand.
I went home and I went straight to my bedroom.
I stayed awake, I was frightened.
Every time I heard a noise, my heart would race.
I would panic.
I thought they would be coming any second to take me away.
All night I sat in bed, shaking, waiting for them to knock.
But they didn't.

Short pause.

BRIAN: Is that why you did it?

Mathew is silent.

BRIAN: Is that why?

MATHEW: I didn't come here to steal.

BRIAN: Did you tell anybody?

MATHEW: No.
My Mum was at work.
My Step Dad was at home and I don't talk to him.
I don't talk to him about anything.

BRIAN: Did you really believe they were going to knock on your door that night?

MATHEW: I was eight.

BRIAN: They don't care.
I've read about them, I've studied them.
They don't care, not near enough.
They do not care for you or me.
Do you understand?

Mathew is silent.

BRIAN: Do you?

MATHEW: Why do you hate the police?

BRIAN: What?
I don't hate police, that's not what I said.

MATHEW: You said / they…

BRIAN: / I said that they could do more, a hell of a lot more.
They could help more.
They don't recognize the real problems, they don't.
They just see an irritant, they don't see the illness.
They see a thorn, but they don't see the pain.
Instead of curing they throw the illness back on to the street and wait for it to spread again.
The illness just gets worse.
Then you can't cure it anymore.
People need help.
And these people express their needs in different ways.
You see these rapists, these murderers, and pedophiles.
They all needed help once too.
The police fail to observe this.
I don't hate the police, I don't.

I have issues with the police, yes.
But I don't hate them.
I don't.

Silence.

MATHEW: I couldn't see the orange sours.

BRIAN: We don't sell them anymore.
People stopped buying them.
We don't order them in.
I haven't sold them for years.

MATHEW: They were my favorite.

Silence.

The Sixth Wave

BRIAN: When I was thirteen, I would go to the beach to listen to the waves.
Each wave holds a different conversation.
I would always look forward to Sundays.
I would do my paper round, and I would finish it as fast as I could, because I knew when I had, I could visit for an hour before my mam called me in for breakfast.
I would stand there and listen.
I would listen to every lingering vowel.
It smiled at me too, made me feel welcome.
It would whisper me secrets.
It told me the seventh wave transports you to the 8th.
It said that one day I would be happy, truly happy.
It made me feel wanted.
It told me it would take me away from this and take me to a place.
Somewhere peaceful it said.
The 8th wave.
It's a place we are taken to after the chaos.
And it told me it would keep me there, forever, wrapped in its embrace.

Mist begins to cover the stage.

BRIAN: And it did.
For a little while.

Mathew begins to piss. It leaks through his trousers onto the floor.

BRIAN: It told me to take off my shoes and socks, so I did.
It told me to take off shirt and trousers and it told me to fold them neatly.

It told me to leave them two meters away from the tide.
So I did.
And I knew this specific morning it was cold, and it was very windy.
I looked around, and the beach was completely empty.
But I wasn't alone.

The piss covers the stage.
The wooden boat begins to grow in size.

BRIAN: The first wave, I made a decision.
Second wave, I went in, it was freezing.
The third, further.
It was so cold, I was gasping for air.
The forth wave, deeper, I kept going until I was surrounded, it was up to here.
The fifth I felt apart of it, like a little grain of sand.
The sixth, I slipped, I went under.
And the seventh, I hit my head.

And there I was, in the mist, lots of mist.
It wasn't suffocating either.
No, it wasn't like the smoke from a cigarette.
It was refreshing.
Every single time I took a deep breath in...
You couldn't see much either.
It was like living inside a cloud, but I wasn't floating.
There was grass on the ground, long, damp grass.
It was cold, but it didn't matter.
It didn't matter that it was cold, I enjoyed it.
It was like a blanket, comforting.

The tide of the water lifts the life-sized boat.

And I lay there.
Inescapably free.
I existed in that moment, and I didn't think of the future, or the past, in fact I didn't think much at all.
After sometime I totally forgot how I got there.
I just lay, on the grass, breathing out haze, adding to the cloud.
Existing.

Short pause.

BRIAN: I arrived back three weeks after.
I opened my eyes and I thought, "Oh, back here again"
A doctor came, saw me, and I was back home soon after that.

Silence.

The Seventh Wave

It is seven o'clock in the morning.
The seagulls have begun to screech outside.
Mathew is now free.
Brian and Mathew are varnishing the wooden boat together.
In the room, there is the old blue suitcase.

BRIAN: Why don't you speak to him?
Your Dad?

MATHEW: My Step Dad.

BRIAN: Did he do something wrong?

MATHEW: I dared him once.
Well, he threatened me first, so then I dared him.
He was my Step Dad, I didn't think he would do it, I mean, why would you do that to a little lad?
But he did.

BRIAN: What did he do?

MATHEW: He took the scissors and he chopped off a chunk.
I loved my hair, sounds such a queer thing to say, but I did.
I've never dared anybody since, because I'm scared if I did, they might just do it.

BRIAN: How old were you?

MATHEW: I don't know.
I just remember going into my bedroom, putting my head over the plastic bin and chopping it all off.

I got the scissors and cut, I was sobbing every step of the way.
I wanted to scream.
I wanted him to hear me screaming.
But I didn't.
I remember looking in the mirror at what I'd done.
I remember looking back down at the bin and then back at the mirror again.
That's when I started laughing, tears were strolling down my face, but I was laughing.
I don't know why I laughed, I looked horrific, but I did.

BRIAN: That's such a sad story.

MATHEW: No, it isn't.
I felt like danger mouse.
I felt indestructible, untouchable.

BRIAN: But you looked horrific.

MATHEW: Yes, but I felt amazing.
When I looked in that mirror I thought, "Fuck. You."

BRIAN: So, that is why you laughed.

They continue to varnish the boat.

MATHEW: Were you a polite kid?

BRIAN: Of course.

MATHEW: Were you needy?

BRIAN: Needy?
Children need to be needy.
Otherwise they would not survive.

MATHEW: Not constantly.

BRIAN: Not constantly no.
But some children do.
Some children clutch onto you.
Like a shadow.
I have seen them drain.
I was never a clutcher.
I was never too needy.
I found the balance rather easily.
Mam always said I was the perfect child.

MATHEW: Really?

BRIAN: Oh yes, in everyway.
Were you somebody's shadow?

MATHEW: No.

BRIAN: Really?
You look like you were somebody's shadow.

MATHEW: I wasn't.
My Brother was a shadow.

BRIAN: Your Mother's shadow?

MATHEW: My shadow.

BRIAN: Was he?
I never had a Brother.

MATHEW: Sisters?

BRIAN: No siblings.

MATHEW: An only child.
And you weren't needy?

BRIAN: As a child, no, I was not.

Short pause.

BRIAN: Did you read to your Brother?

MATHEW: I did.

BRIAN: What would you read?

MATHEW: Books.

BRIAN: What type of / books?

MATHEW: / Different, different types of / books.

BRIAN: Good books?

MATHEW: I liked them.

Brian Did you read articles too?

MATHEW: No.

BRIAN: Did the stories have morals?

MATHEW: What?

BRIAN: Did your Brother learn things from the stories you told him?

MATHEW: I'm not sure.

BRIAN: Is he smart?

MATHEW: Yes, he is.
Much smarter than me.

Brian smiles.

BRIAN: So, he learnt the morals from the stories that you told him.

Short pause.

BRIAN: Did you cook for him too?

MATHEW: Yes.

BRIAN: Play?

MATHEW: With him, yes.

BRIAN: Clean?

MATHEW: Sometimes.

BRIAN: Make the bed?

MATHEW: No.

BRIAN: You never made the bed?

MATHEW: No, my Mother never made her bed.

BRIAN: Right.
Well, that must have been rather / difficult.

MATHEW: / It was hard, sometimes.

BRIAN: I bet he loves you very much.

MATHEW: Yes, he does.

BRIAN: You're a good brother.
Where is he now?

MATHEW: He doesn't live at home anymore.

BRIAN: So, where is he?

MATHEW: He moved away.

BRIAN: Where did he move / to?

MATHEW: / Away.

Short pause.

MATHEW: I remember tucking him into bed at seven.
I remember reading him stories.
The ones...
The goat one and the one about the bridge, he liked that one.
When he shut his eyes, I would place the book on the floor, turn off the light and walk downstairs.
I would sit on the chair in the back garden and I would smoke.

My step dad sold the stuff, skunk.
Everyday around 8pm I would sit there.
My mind would stop running around in circles.
I sat there, eyes glazed, hearing on mute.
I wouldn't think of tomorrow.
I would imagine, and dream and I would somehow, feel in...
Some things I thought I would / never...

BRIAN: / Did you cry?

MATHEW: Sometimes I did, yes.

Brian smiles.
Brian takes two cigarettes from his pocket.
He gives one cigarette to Mathew.

BRIAN: I understand.

They smoke.

MATHEW: Can I tell you something?

BRIAN: Of Corse.

MATHEW: You won't tell / anyone.

BRIAN: / I won't.

MATHEW: I still do it.
I sit there on his bed, and I read the story.
I turn off the light and I sit in the chair in the back garden.
I know it's silly because he isn't there, but I still do it.

The seagulls screech.

Silence.

BRIAN: I want to give you my keys.
To the shop.

MATHEW: You what?

BRIAN: You heard me.
You want to look after the shop?

MATHEW: Yes.

Brian takes the keys from his pocket.
Brian holds them out in front of Mathew.

BRIAN: Take them.

Mathew takes the keys from Brian's hand.

BRIAN: Right, think fast, think sharp.
There are four keys.
The red one is for the back door.
The little grey one if for the shed outside.
The long black one is for the front and the white one is my bedroom.
Got it.

MATHEW: Got it.

BRIAN: And you will sleep in here and you won't go into my bedroom.
Got it?

MATHEW: Yes.

BRIAN: And you will look after it.
Clean it.
Care for it.
Tend to it, nicely.

MATHEW: I will.

BRIAN: You will look after it.
You won't steal, if you break something, you replace it.
And if anybody asks who put you in charge, you say Brian.
Got it.
You say Brian put me in charge.
Go it.
You tell them / Brian…

MATHEW: / Brian said.

BRIAN: Yes!
Yes, Brian says.

MATHEW: I won't disappoint you.

BRIAN: No, you won't.
It's time.

Seagulls are heard piercingly.
They are focused.
Brian walks over to the suitcase.
He picks the suitcase up.
Brian looks at the boat.
He admires his work.
Sound of seagulls.
Grating.

BRIAN: I lied.

MATHEW: What?

BRIAN: I'm sorry.
I shouldn't have lied.

Short pause.

BRIAN: He didn't come back home that night.
The night with the boat.
He didn't come home.
I went bed and I waited.
The door didn't open.
The next morning I went down stairs, and I asked where Dad was, Mam didn't answer.
I left the boat on the kitchen table and I wrote a little note for him and I left for school.
The bell rang I and rushed home after school, and the boat was still there, on the table, with the letter, it hadn't moved.
I remember going up to his bedroom and all his stuff had gone, I never saw that conch shell again.
And my Dad never came back.

Short pause.

BRIAN: See you soon Mathew.

Brian exits.
Sound of seagulls.
Too loud.
Painful.

Mathew smokes.
He walks over to the boat and climbs inside.
Silence.

The 8th Wave

A room.
There is a light, shining.
It is buzzing.
The light is bright but it flickers a little.
A dentist's chair or a hospital bed.
Perhaps the bed of the sand, deep beneath the waters.
A room underwater.
The boat floats above the waters.
The sound of waves.
Brian is lying down.
Brian is wearing his blue pajamas.
The ones from his suitcase.
His favorite.

There is a beeping.
It is constant.

Beep.

Beep.

Beep.

Beep.

Brian's blue suitcase lies beside him.
It is open.
Sea grass grows out of the suitcase.
The sea grass floats upwards, hypnotically.
It clings to the walls of the room.
It wraps itself around Brian.
Brian has his eyes closed.
He is breathing, slowly.

A little too slow.
We can hear his breath.
We can see it also.

Mathew sits beside him on a chair.
The sea grass tangles itself around the chair legs and around the feet of Mathew.

Mathew is wearing a suit.
Dark blue.
A nice one.
Brand new shoes.

Mathew is holding Brian's hand.
Mathew looks calm.

Beep

Beep.

Beep

The light begins to grow, so does the buzzing.
The light is now flickering regularly.
It creates an uncomfortable feeling.

BRIAN: Its too cold.

MATHEW: I expected it to be.
I knew it would be.

BRIAN: I…
I…
I want you to know that…

MATHEW: I needed to know that.

The beeping becomes faster and higher in pitch.
Brian starts to struggle.
Mathew tries to comfort Brian.
Brian tries to sit upwards.
Mathew pushes Brian's chest down onto the bed.
The light begins to grow brighter and flicker, quicker.
Violent.
The buzzing grows.
It becomes far too loud.
Almost painful.

The beeping is now constant.
Even higher in pitch.
Much like a sound of a drill at the dentist.
It is attacking.

Beeeeeeeeeeeeeeeeeeeeeeeeeeeeeeeeeeeeeeeeeeeeeeeeeeeeeeeeeeeeeeeeeep.

Silence.

A strong bright light.
The sound of waves.
Brian begins to float.
Peacefully.
After sometime, the light fades, slowly, to darkness.
End.